Take My Hand

PHYSICAL GUIDED ACTION

Tony LoBue

Math. 19: 13 -14

BY TONY LOBUE

A new approach to guide children toward better behavior.

ACKNOWLEDGEMENT

My sincere appreciation to Barbara Burke for proof reading the book and to my wife Georgia for her patience and support during the writing of this book

Library of Congress Catalogue #89-90531
ISBN# 0-9625492-0-7

ACARE PUBLISHERS
358 Sierra Vista Drive
Aptos, California 95003

Printed in the United States of America
Book Design & Typography by Type & Design, Scotts Valley, California

*To the memory of
LARRY
and all the other young
people who might have
benefitted from the
information in this book*

TERMS

I would like to define some of the concepts and coined phrases used in the book, to assist in your reading comprehension.

PHYSICAL GUIDED ACTION, (PGA): a process to assist children through fears, new experiences, misjudgements and misbehavior where the end result is caring behavior, inner strength and appropriate behavior.

CARING BEHAVIOR: behavior with many outward characteristics; among them are being cooperative, helpful, supportive, sensitive, loyal, thoughtful, giving or any other characteristics the reader may identify as showing "care" for another person.

CENTERING ON THE CHILD: to give the child undivided attention in an attempt to completely understand and deal with his needs.

COGNITIVE CONCEIT: a child's interpretation of adults as being so weak that he the child thinks he is extra powerful over himself, adults and life in general.

HEALTHY RISK: a child having the confidence to try similar or new events in his life.

CONTENTS

INTRODUCTION

"This class doesn't seem too bad" "You stay off my back, and I'll keep off yours." "My name is Larry, and I am known as a thief." These words were written to me by a seventeen year old boy on his first day of school. Larry was right, he was a thief; but he was also an intelligent, loyal, feeling and caring person. Somewhere along Larry's life, he had accumulated many negative experiences, dictating an image of low character. He was a brilliant youngster, yet his fight between who he really was and what he had programmed himself to be, constantly confused him. Let me, if I may, tell you briefly about the real Larry.

I had taken a new teaching assignment in the mid-sixties, that enriched my life in many ways. My students were all on juvenile probation, and one step from CYA placement (California Youth Authority—Institution for serious juvenile offenders.) This newly organized community treatment program was an approach to treating juvenile deliquents in an attempt to avoid placing them in CYA. Larry walked into class with a defiant strut, escorted by his probation officer. He cautiously looked around the room, examining every detail. In a short time he established a non-verbal leaderhsip among the other students. Like some magical power, there was an unspoken rule communicated by Larry throughout the class. He could quickly manipulates the mood of the class with a commanding look. My biggest job in this new position was to gain Larry's trust. We seemed to build our trust best in two ways; through notes written to each other on English compositions; and by doing unrequested things for each other. Larry's pattern was to throw smoke screens at me by writing statements in his compositions to elicit a reaction. (A smoke screen is a statement or behavior to check out the adult, and see if it is safe to reveal the real pain.) Larry would make a statement like, "all white men raped and used my sisters and brothers." Larry's statement was to check out with me if it was safe to tell about the anger and confusion, and pain he was having with his life, especially that connected with trust. He loved soul music, and he had the wonderful and gifted wit to make us all laugh. How quick he could be to see the lighter side of things. The second way we built our trust was to do things for each other without being asked. Asking Larry for assistance was interpreted by him as control or manipulation, and this did not go well at all. He was extremely sensitive to fairness and used assertive actions to bring that to class events. This was first shown to me when a new student entered my class about mid-year. On his second day in class the new student pulled out a switch blade knife and commenced to flip the blade open and closed. This bchavior was donc during a class discussion on history in an attempt to establish power and significance in the class. I had a tendency to jump on intolerable behavior quickly, so I stopped my lesson and requested that he put the knife back in his pocket. Our new student looked up at me with those defiant eyes and continued to open and close the blade. Digging a little bit deeper into my authoritarian background, I squared off, and repeated my requested to put the knife away. This time the defiant eye response was accompanied by the words, "What are you going to do if I don't" Larry must have sensed that I had run out of wisdom in controlling delinquent behavior, and before I could say another word, Larry, from the back of the room, said, "Put that blade away." Our new student, almost like magic, transformed into the most cooperative member of the class. He quickly put his knife away, never to take it out for the rest of the school year. I took a deep swallow and continued the discussion while my heart slowly returned to a normal state.

Larry's loyalty had to be under his control and so did mine. He frequently complained about the poor housing he and his brother, sister, and mother lived in. Larry did not come to school one day, and I learned that Larry and his entire family were in the hospital. They had been asphyxiated in their rented home due to a faulty gas valve. When I went to the hospital, Larry and his family were all in the same room. It was my first time to meet his family and Larry, although still very sick, made all the introductions and attempted to cheer everyone. I remember clearly the frightened eyes looking at me over those white sheets. I made the mistake of asking Larry if there was anything I could do for his family. He shook his head, "no," and gave me the stern assuring look that I had already done what was needed.

7

Larry did so well academically and socially that he returned to his regular high school for his senior year. He made occasional visits to my one room school to say hello and "check" if I was doing my job. He always brought with him a new friend to introduce to me.

I wish Larry's story could continue on an upward spiral, but unfortunately Larry was killed by the very same elements in his life that made him feel so angry and untrusting. One late afternoon he was playing pool by himself when a group of Hell's Angels entered the pool hall and demanded the use of his table. Larry was roughed up and forced out of the pool hall. Minutes later Larry returned with some friends and a gang fight broke out. During the fight Larry was fatally shot by one of the Hell's Angels and died one week later in a community hospital.

Larry's story that I have shared with you has been one of the incentives in motivating me to write this book. We all lost someone special when we lost Larry. Here was a Jewel that got lost in the web of revenge, hatred, pain and mistreatment. We have lost many Jewels in this world, and it must stop, for I believe that they hold some of the keys to the future for all of us. But, there is something we can do, and that is to encourage the God-given goodness and greatness in each child. Children need guildance in their lives, in doing what is right. Reflecting back on Larry's first day of school with me, I cannot help but wonder how his life could have been different if he had been guided in such a way that he identified himself as the intelligent, loyal, feeling, and caring person he was, instead of a thief.

The purpose of this book is to give adults who work with children the skills to change negative attitudes and behavior in children.

The Foundational Base For Discipline

Raising children, in a sense, is like raising roses. When we allow roses to grow wild without pruning them, we have a plant that spends much of its energy growing cellulose material...producing few or no blossoms.

Dad goes to work Monday morning still exhausted from the disappointing time he had at the company's weekend, family picnic. Bobby, the youngest of his three children, presented quite a problem. Spitting food at his oldest brother resulted in Dad spanking Bobby in front of the entire staff of fellow workers. What made it worse was that Bobby ran away from Dad screaming "I hate you" at the top of his lungs. Of course, this caused Dad to feel like he had lost complete control over Bobby. Also, his pride as a good father went right down the tubes. The words, "I hate you", also brought Dad to a second level of anger and his next move was to chase Bobby, yank him by the arm and give him one more good wallop on the posterior end. Dad at this time was so embarrassed that he ended the picnic for his entire family and went home.

We can easily conclude that this family scenario is much too painful and familiar to many of us. Raising children, in a sense, is like raising roses. When we allow roses to grow wild without pruning them, we then have a plant that spends much of its energy growing cellulose material which produces a lot of cane growth, but few or no blossoms. In order to assist the rose to produce blossoms we must prune away the dead wood and excess cane growth. This is also true with disciplining children. Often, as they are developing, they do things that are inappropriate and harmful to themselves and others. We must, as the adults in their lives, prune or respond in a way that will motivate the child to change that behavior. On the other hand, over-disciplining, like over pruning, may discourage positive growth. Unfortunately, just like the rose bush and its thorns, we get pricked in the process, causing us to feel anger and hurt. Children are quite often very proficient in their ability to "hurt back" when we are in the process of pruning away inappropriate behavior. Their thorns are in the form of hurtful words such as "I hate you," "you are the worst mom, dad, teacher!!!" "Did you know no one in this class likes the way you teach," "My last year's teacher never gave me less than an 'A'," or "John's mom lets him stay up past 10:00 p.m."

Words are not only meant to hurt the adult but also to manipulate the situation to gain an upper hand. On the other hand, sometimes the thorn is a subtle rejection such as pushing the adult away or not talking to the adult. Out of revenge, a child may destroy something the adult valued or a special gift given to the child. This behavior is meant to purposely hurt the adult.

Just as when we are stuck once too often by a rose thorn, we may react immediately and with strong emotion when we are hurt by our children, overreacting and disciplining too severely. For the child this acting too severely may lead to emotional scarring.

Just as the rose may not produce blossoms, the child may submerge the God-given talents and traits that foster inward and outward emotional peace. As parents and teachers, our goal in correcting children is to change behavior.

Much too often in counseling sessions I have listened to clients describe incidents of punishment in their lives which left clear memories and imprints of the punishment act itself. When asked what the punishment was for, they often could not remember the details of the behavior being corrected.

Yakack is a Hebrew word which when translated means to "reason together." The word "reason" implies that in the discipline process we should be listening, pointing out error and giving direction to the child. Using a gentle tone, discipline is a way of setting limits, as a demonstration of the adult's love for that child. When a child cannot remember what he has done to deserve punishment, but only the punishment itself, then it is possible that the discipline process was so severe that it anchored into the child's memory bank the profound details of the punishment act. It is possible for children to remember details, such as the adult's arrow piercing eyes, exact sounds made by the adult, words that attacked the child's character such as "what a stupid thing you did." Even smells and hurtful touches can long be remembered and recalled into adult life. Unfortunately, children spend many years using energy to overcome the hurt associated with the punishment act instead of growing and maturing with new skills that assist them in making good decisions.

We tend to associate discipline with punishment, believing that our action toward the child should hurt! Unfortunately we have misunderstood that discipline means to instruct or guide. The word "discipline" comes from the word "disciple" implying that there is a learner and a teacher. In whatever capacity we find ourselves, whether it be as a parent or school teacher, we are the ones responsible for the teaching. If only a manual could precede the newborn baby, telling us in detail much about his personality traits: we might prepare ourselves to raise the child with less pain. There is no "teacher" on earth who has ever raised or taught a child without needing time, patience, energy and lots of rest and relaxation!!

MOST COMMON DISCIPLINE BREAKDOWNS

Adults assisting children in any capacity love to feel satisfied with their involvement in teaching their child. Positive feedback to the teacher encourages him to risk more with the youngster's learning. The teacher's self-esteem is greatly influenced by the child's positive behavioral changes. It is important, then, to describe the most common breakdowns associated with the discipline processes used by adults.

THE ADULT'S CONFIDENCE IN THE EYES OF THE CHILD

An adult's lack of self-confidence contributes to a low sense of protection and security for the child. When adults show a lack of reliance in their judgement, the phenomenon of *cognitive conceit* in the child's development with the adult world is increased. The child interprets that if the parent feels so unsure of what to do, then the child must know more than the parent. The cognitive conceit phenomenon in the case of the unsure adult usually result in frustration, anxiety and low self-esteem by the child. Let's face it, adults are going to make many mistakes in handling children. The healthiest way to handle such mistakes is to be honest with the child, show how you have corrected the mistake (this is setting a model for the child to handle his mistakes), and then go on with assurance. If the adult does not know what to do in a particular behavioral situation, then it is best to say, "At this time I really do not know what to say to you about your behavior. I need some time to think about this and I promise I will talk to you within fifteen minutes." The adult must be in charge of the child and establish guidance and direction for him. It is important to remind ourselves that we must tolerate the fact that we are not perfect. Failures and successes are part of everyone's life. In fact, failure quite often opens up the avenues to real growth.

CONSISTENCY
IN GUIDANCE

The second most common breakdown in disciplining children is the adult's *lack of consistency.* Guiding children is not supposed to be like riding a roller coaster. The rules within any environment must be the same tomorrow as they are today. Most children, because of their need for self-gratification, attempt to change and bend the rules. Let us give then an "A" for effort, but the rule stays the same! Consistency in all adult behaviors that contribute to the child's emotional wellness is essential. The child that feels that he is loved is also feeling he is a worthwhile person no matter if he gets an "A" or a "D" in math. Nurturing and environmental structuring should always be available for the child. Our most noted deficiency as adults is our lack of availability for our children. With the tremendous stress parents and teachers are presently experiencing in the eighties we must find a way to recuperate and maintain quality time with our children. Children today are receiving an average of seven to fifteen minutes of personal quality time from their parents daily. Lack of consistency in both controlling and supporting any youngster produces future adults with confused and unstable life goals.

ESTABLISHING CLARITY WITH THE CHILD
WITHOUT DESTROYING CHARACTER

Disciplining children also requires being clear in what we want the child to do. Lack of clear communication in parent-child relationships is a common problem in many families. Children, during their early years of development see the world differently than adults do. Just consider how the adult and four-year old view the following situation: Billy invites his neighbor friend over to his home to play. Mother observes that her son refuses to let his friend use his tricycle while they are playing. Mother becomes concerned about Billy's resistance to sharing and steps in with a directive to let his friend have a turn riding the tricycle. Billy allows mother to give the tricycle to the friend but runs to his room screaming. When we look closer at the behavioral interpretation of what took place, we see two different views of Billy's resistance in sharing the tricycle. One, mother views her son's resistant behavior as selfishness. Her motivation to get Billy to share the tricycle was to encourage the friendship through an act of sharing. Billy has a completely different view of his resistance. Holding on to his tricycle is like holding on to a part of himself. In his reasoning, giving up the tricycle is like giving up a part of himself. Looking through the eyes of our children is vital when constructively directing them. I believe this difference in viewpoint between adults and children lasts until the child has accumulated enough experiences to fully understand cause and affect in human behavior.

As we train our children and correct behavior our words should avoid any negative descriptions of the child's image as a person. When correcting a child, it does not help to use words such as selfish, lazy or sloppy. For children, these words are understood as disapproval of "self" and not the child's behavior. It is suggested that as we address this issue of clarity we stress clear statements of what we want the child to do without the use of negative words that attack the youngster's character.

In the case of Billy not wanting to share his tricycle, it would have been best for the parent not to view Billy's resistance to sharing as a misbehavior but to see it as more of a developmental process Billy and his friend must go through themselves. There is a common understanding among children when they deal with issues of cooperation and sharing. This understanding is somewhat foreign to adults because of the distance created by the experiential development of the adult. Adults, after rising to higher levels of cognitive thinking and reasoning, tend to leave behind or extinguish the reasoning earlier experienced as a child. For this reason it would have been best for mom to let Billy and his friend work out the arrangement of sharing the tricycle between themselves. It is amazing what children do work out without adult's direct assistance. We are quite certain that youngsters may learn more about regulating human relationships through the rules they make among themselves in play, than by the rules set down by adults. Children then understand the value of their parents' rules when they have been reinforced by the rules they have made among their peers.

CONSEQUENCES, FAIRNESS AND FOLLOW-THROUGH

Another common breakdown in the discipline process is the

adult's failure to fit the consequence of a misbehavior with the misbehavior itself. It is very easy to overpunish when our children drive us to high levels of anger. The act of over-punishing is normally preceded by the adult becoming emotionally frustrated with the child. Let us say that Jimmy, a fourth grader, has learned to question everything his teacher directs the class to do. Jimmy unfortunately understands that the only way he really counts in the world is to be more powerful than those around him. Therefore he questions those in authority hoping for an argument or debate. With children like Jimmy, adults have a tendency to punish (too severely.) "Okay" states the teacher, "you have just bought yourself five hundred lines of I will not open my mouth until I am twenty-one years old."

On the other hand, if we set up certain consequences with the child we must follow through and not find ourselves negotiating over the behavior or consequence. Best "rule of thumb" within the home environment is to set up reasonable consequences before the misbehavior ever occurs. I do not feel it is always necessary to inform our children of these consequences. I base this withholding of consequence on two reasons. First, the message "if you are late coming home you will lose the privilege of going to your friends house for one week" implies that the child is irresponsible before he has shown irresponsibility. It is like always reminding the child to be good. Second, it now gives the child the alternative to misbehave, which many children choose to do. If the child comes home late validate what this tardy behavior has done to you (made you worry, held up dinner, etc.) and then state the consequence for the behavior. (I will describe the Physical Guided Action process which could also be used with the consequences in a later chapter.) Reasonable action and fewer words are both healthier for and respected by the child. If the child repeats the misbehavior of being late then follow through with the same consequences again. We often give up too early with consequences because the child continually repeats the misbehavior. Just when the child is approaching changes in behavior we give up and start using different consequences. Some of our children, by the way in which genetics played a part in their personalities, are going to be hard to raise. Let us not give up the ship because it doesn't always sail smoothly. Don't give up on a method just because it doesn't work at first. We may have to use correctional procedures many times before we observe positive change in a child's behavior. Interestingly, research suggests that specific consequences that work best in altering misbehavior cannot be identified. Behavioral changes in youngsters are influenced more by the consistency, follow through and fairness of the consequence, than by the type of consequence administered.

MISBEHAVIOR AS PART OF A CHILD'S GROWTH

Misbehavior in children is neither good nor bad, rather it seems to be a vehicle which they use to grow both intellectually and emotionally. Each child has an important meaning to his existence on this earth. It seems that part of the process for discovering this meaning in life comes from trial and errors in the child's behavior.

The child first enters the world totally dependent on the providers in his home environment. The child knows no limits to his behavior. He cries when he is hungry or uncomfortable, and he achieves instant gratification from the provider. The provider at this time in the child's life seldom exercises rules or conditions for approval.

There are, of course, providers who are mentally illequipped to raise a child and do not fit the above description. Instead of meeting the child's needs they are occupied in trying to cope with their own emotional pathology. The children of these parents, unfortunately are psychologically harmed for many years. This is why we observed these children struggling while working on school tasks. Their subconscious minds are often focused on problems or events which occurred outside of the school setting. The child who becomes emotionally disturbed due to inconsistent or negative nurturing does not follow the normal emotional development pattern described in this chapter.

By the time the child reaches the age of two he has developed a conscience which informs him that the world has limits. This becomes frustrating to the child for he does not have the mental reasoning skill to fully comprehend this change in his life. The child's sense of belonging is now tempered with conditions. For example, when two year old Tommy takes his crayon and draws circles and lines all over his bedroom wall he most likely will receive disapproval from mom and dad. The approval and disapproval responses by the parent-teacher assist in developing new behaviors to secure the sense of belonging within the child's environment. Quite often the concept of approval-disapproval is the motivator to promote positive and negative changes.

To hold on to a sense of high self-esteem and inner strength the child, between the ages to two to five, resorts to the use of fantasy. This is done quite often to establish connection with the adult world. Little Ray, who is five years old, visits frequently with the adult next door. He sophisticatedly tells the neighbor how he is going to the South Pole to visit the penguins. Fantasy is not a form of misbehavior nor should it be viewed as a serious mental disturbance. The child will need assistance in sharing some new interest and information about the South Pole and a living creature that lives there. A healthy response from the adult might go like this: "Gee Ray you have really learned alot about penguins. Let's go look at a map and find where the South Pole is." A frequent mistake by adults toward child fantasies is to tell the child he is not telling the truth. This is quite often followed by a lecture about being honest. The most famous resource story told by the adult in these cases is "The Little Boy Who Called Wolf." Fantasy with children is perfectly natural and serves to place the child in an active mind experience with the world. A child may not be able to physically experience doing something or being a certain person. In fantasy, he fulfills the desire to do something by using his imaginative powers. Fantasy also serves as a way to resolve conflict or losses by the child. For example, the child might fantasize that he is related to a female or male movie star to replace the love and attention of a deceased parent.

To reinforce what was stated earlier, fantasy by children should be treated in such a way that we as the adults assist the child to use the fantasy in sorting out the contents of his life that are real. It is exciting and rewarding to a child to imagine himself to be someone else. Fantasies may well be part of the process through which children ultimately find themselves and realize the essence of their existence on earth.

By the time the child enters school (five to six years old) he has already learned there is a serious side to life. He starts to sense a "closing-in" on his freedom by rules that bombard him from every direction. Remember, the child did not start in his world this way. There were no rules which forbade crying as an infant. This was the child's behavior that brought about fulfillment of a need.

Entering school introduces the element of control: control in moving about the room at free will; control in talking or expressing needs; control in the type of involvement he can have with others and control in the use of exploring his interest. This writer certainly does not want to lead the reader to believe that these controls are all bad for children to adjust to, but more to make the reader view with better understanding what the child is adjusting to. The vast amount of adjustment and compliance to rules and controls is not always easy for children. Some children by the nature of their own inherited congenital temperaments are going to have more difficulty adapting to rules than others. Quite often misbehavior in some children will increase when they enter school. Again, it is the adult's job to understand what is happening to the child and then to bring this understanding to an awareness level where the child can understand what's happening to him. How many times have we asked children why they did what they did, only to receive back the answer "I don't know why I did that." I believe children, many times do not know why they misbehave. When anyone is suffering for lack of significance and belonging to a family or classroom full of personally unattached people, he is often involved in behavior that is not premeditated or thought out. The misbehavior is often a symptom of confusion, fear and panic directly related to a desire to feel personal worth and belonging. As the child grows in age this confusion increases in proportion to the child's lack of ability to learn how to cope with his world.

Learning to cope with the world is one crucial area for which we as adults often fail to prepare our children. Coping means that the child must first understand how his behavior affects others. Second, he needs to know why people react to his behavior as they do. Third, what was it that the child really wanted to accomplish with the behavior? (attention, participation, friendship, comfort, etc.) Fourth, what new skills can the child learn and use that help him accomplish or fulfill the same need that would be more appropriate? Most of the time, the need behind the misbehavior is not wrong. It is the action which the child chose to gratify the need that is destructive to mental wellness.

Let's visit with little Ray again and examine carefully how these coping skills can assist little Ray with a second grade problem.

There are those in second grade who love to build sand castles and those that love to stomp them down. Well, little Ray happens to be a stomper. Little Ray and Billy are brought to the office for throwing sand at each other. Ray is crying because he got sand thrown in his face and Billy can't talk or cry, because he had a mouth full of sand fed to him by little Ray. When the adult asked what happened both boys had agreeable explanations of what occurred. Little Ray agreed that he did jump and crash down Billy's sand castle.

Adult:	"Looks like you got alot of sand on your face Ray."
Little Ray:	"I don't like Billy because he's mean.'
Adult:	"It sounds like you were mad at Billy before you jumped on his castle."
Little Ray:	"Yeah, he stinks."
Adult:	"You're still angry at Billy."
Little Ray:	"He never lets me play with him."
Adult:	"When you broke Billy's castle you were really trying to get him to let you play with him." "Do you want Billy to be your friend?" (Awareness of Little Ray's needs)
Little Ray:	"Only if he lets me play with him."
Adult:	"Ask Billy if he would like to be your friend."
Little Ray:	"Billy, do you want to be my friend?"
Billy:	"Only if you stop pushing and jumping all over my back."
Adult:	"Billy, it sounds like it would be easier to be Ray's friend if he treated you more gently." "Ray, I believe you really want Billy to like you, not to be mad at you. Is that right?"
Little Ray:	Yes.
Adult:	"Do you know of another way you could get Billy's attention so that he could feel happy with you?" (New skill to accomplish same need)

Let's stop with the adult's last questions for Little Ray to ponder over and examine the misbehavior which was used to fulfill a very important need. (Refer to Diagram 1.0)

ANGER	HURT	EXPECTATIONS	NEEDS
Anger is experienced in Ray's aggressive behavior; (jumping on castle.)	Behind Ray's anger is the hurt of rejection caused by Ray's poor skills to relate or make friends.	Behind Ray's hurt was anticipation or expectation for friendship.	Behind Ray's expectations are needs to skillfully make friends and ultimately receive positive feedback and companionship from peers.

DIAGRAM 1.0

The last question asked by the adult "Do you know another way which you could get Billy to be your friend?" was directing Ray to focus on new skills to achieve the universal need of belonging.

Many children, like Ray, simply do not know how to skillfully change their behavior to fulfill their needs. We, as the adults, must help children change their behavior. The main emphasis by the adult should be to move toward the need area of the child rather than to focus solely on the misbehavior (symptom.)

CHAPTER SUMMARY

Misbehavior is basically a natural process for children to learn how to live within their world. The adult's prime job in reacting to the misbehavior is to understand the needs of the child and teach him better ways to fulfill these needs. Besides stating consequences for misbehavior, there is actual teaching of skills that must be included in the discipline process for children. The discipline methods used by adults should emphasize guidance as opposed to only punishment.

There is a natural gap between an adult's and child's perception of the world. Adults need to be cautious not to place unrealistic expectations upon the child's behavior. Adults are the child's main support as they are emerging into adulthood themselves. Time with the child is essential now. Time actively invested *now* results in a child who will lead a responsible, morally productive and happy life in the future.

Successfully re-experiencing a previously negative situation, using new skills, helps to build self-esteem and inner strength.

Much too often adults discipline children by focusing only on the symptom (i.e., the misbehavior) rather than the need. We have incorrectly concluded that if we just get the child to stop the misbehavior then we have accomplished our job.

Maintaining a Balance Between Control and Support In a Child's Environment

Usually an environment where there is less conflict and more caring is one that maintains a balance of control and support.

There would be little disagreement about how most adults would like to spend the majority of their time with children. Most school teachers would agree that days in the classroom with little need to discipline and high student cooperation are days of satisfaciton. Parents, too, enjoy being around their children when there is less conflict and more harmony within the home. Harmony among children and the ensuing satisfaction among parents and teachers is possible at home and school. Usually an environment where there is less conflict and more caring is one that maintains a balance of control and support among all of its members. Let us look at both of these elements within the environment.

Control In The Environment = the ability to motivate the child to do "what is right."

There are two types of control that people exhibit in their behavior. The first type is called *help control*. Help control is where the child requires outside assistance in limiting certain behaviors. If, for instance, a jar of candy is conveniently placed in the child's reach he is most likely going to indulge in the sweets until either he becomes physically sick, the adults says "no more candy," and/or the candy is removed from sight. Children seek pleasure and gratification first. It is only when we help control the gratification through physical actions such as removing candy or limiting its use that we put off instant gratification and teach self-control. Unfortunately, we witness adults in our society that still need help control to keep them from manipulating or hurting others. Our prisons are full of people who can only function when an outsider is carefully watching over their behavior. Help control is a part of every young child's life. This type of control is an introduction to self-control in every child's life so that, he may safely reach a level of maturity and understanding of the world around him.

The second type of control we observe in people is *self-control*. This control is motivated from within and results in the child/adult being able to function with others at a high level of productivity. This control is what we hope to guide our children towards in the Physical Guided Action (PGA) process. (To be discussed in a later chapter)

Self control has distinct stages in it's development. The child first needs *direct physical guidance* within his home environment. Self-control starts with the adult's managing of activities in the home. Managing, in this sense, does not mean to limit every aspect of the child's natural curiosity. Rather, it means to guide children so that they learn to stop when their behavior can hurt themselves or others. Children do not enter the world with built in inhibitors. The three-year old youngster who is having a great time throwing a ball back and forth with his dad does not want to stop to get ready for bed. The parent has to supply direct control in situations such as this.

As the child grows into his elementary school years (ages 5-12) self-control is influenced both by direct and indirect actions by the adult. Direct means the adult is still responsible for managing the child's environment, but, is starting to use indirect clues to motivate self-control by the child. Giving indirect clues, means that the adult takes on more of a coaching behavior. This could be compared to the young teenager behind the steering wheel actually driving the car with the adult taking a coaching role. Children at this time of their lives demonstrate much self-control when their parents have established clearly defined rules. Rules can stop children from behaving inappropriately when they realize that rules are useful and breaking them result in consistent, negative consequences. Beyond rules there are many other indirect clues that help children to exercise self-control. (Refer to Table A)

It is important to balance all control with support. Support, provides an environment where the child feels accepted, valued and loved.

SUPPORT

Support always starts with the providers (teacher-parents) supporting one another. Sever conflict among providers destroys the youngster's sense of security and protection. Much has already been written about marital bonding so I will not elaborate, but only point out that without it the youngster today cannot live with the inner confidence he needs to live in an already troubled world.

Children equally look up to their teachers for support in the elementary school years. I would like to identify some characteristics of teachers' behaviors I have observed that benefit children. (Refer to Table B.)

TABLE A
INDIRECT CLUES THAT MOTIVATE AND INCREASE SELF-CONTROL

1. EYE CONTACT:

An adult look reflecting that the behavior must stop. The adult's eyes do not reflect hostility towards child, but rather a concern for child.

2. TOUCH:

A touch on the shoulder or arm that is firm but not painful. The touch should tell the child "I care for you so much I do not want you to continue this behavior."

3. PHYSICAL CLOSENESS WITHOUT TOUCH:

Moving physically close to the child. No words are spoken but your closeness motivates the child to stop negative behavior and draws attention back to desired behavior.

4. PHYSICAL CLOSENESS WITH TOUCH:

This clue is basically doing the opposite of what the child expected you to do. It works wonders with a child who is seeking attention from siblings or classmates while the adult is trying to gain their attention. The adult moves toward the child or has the child come to him, and then with an arm around the child draws him close. It works wonders with kindergarten to third graders. No words are used that reflect disappointment in the child's misbehavior.

5. RECOGNIZING POSITIVE MODELS:

This indirect clue is used to bring attention to the behavior that is appropriate to the present situation. The adult recognizes the child or children who are behaving appropriately with a positive statement, such as, "Thank you for getting your math papers out. I can see you are ready to start."

6. WRISTWATCH TECHNIQUE:

Simply stop, look at your watch and state: "How long will it take for all of us to beat the clock?" The children love the challenge of lowering the amount of time it takes them to gain silence. Next, record time on a corner of the blackboard. This technique can also be used at home with sibling arguments.

7. HAND GESTURES:
A technique that is universally used to bring about direction and control. Common gestures include: Index finger to lips; waving two fingers in air with children imitating gesture; clapping hands twice.

8. INDIRECT MESSAGES:
There are statements that validate how the child's or children's behavior is affecting you. "It makes me feel angry when people are talking while I am giving instructions."

9. PERSONAL SIGNALS:
The teacher or parent works out a hand signal with the child in a private session. For example, the child will know that when he sees his teacher or parent make a "T" with her hands this means that the child is to take some Time Out (a minute or so) and reflect on what he should be doing.

10. IDENTIFY AND GROW:
Identify one aspect of the child's behavior that was positive and then give him the next step.

EXAMPLE

For example, let us say that you have a youngster who is having a dispute with another child over a ball. During the dispute this youngster holds tightly on to the ball explaining that it is his ball and he wants to take it outside. In the process of resisting the other youngster without the ball, he pushes the child away with his shoulder. Your assistance in the case would start with identifying the positive behavior: "Billy, you did a nice job trying to explain that you want control over what belongs to you. Your next step might be to let Sammy know what you are planning to do with your ball."

Again, you refrain from directly controlling the child's behavior. You have allowed the child to take control by giving him some credibility, and then indirectly guiding him to another appropriate behavior. The child may or may not take the next step suggested, but you have reestablished a safe environment for both children. In other words, you have replaced the use of physical aggression with the use of assertive but fair dialogue between the children.

TABLE B
CHARACTERISTICS OF TEACHERS' BEHAVIORS WHICH AFFECT CHILDREN POSITIVELY

1. **ADULTS CARING FOR EACH OTHER:**
   Children get so much joy seeing teachers hug and encourage one another. It is almost magical watching the child's face light up when they watch people they care about caring for one another.

2. **GREETING WITH A PERSONAL COMPLIMENT:**
   Children love to be recognized.
   "You make my day, Mary, every time I see your beautiful smile."
   "Here's my boy, Jimmy, right on time."
   "My day is complete when you're here, Sally."
   "Give me five, Rocky. Heard you did swell in the soccer game last Saturday."
   "Good morning, Bill, it's wonderful to see you."
   "Mornin' to ya', Carey, I'm so glad you are in my class."
   "Love that sweater Sophie."
   "Here's my responsible helper. Hi, David."
   When children are greeted each morning at the classroom door it begins to create a supportive atmosphere for them. The use of complimentary greeting eases the child's need to draw unnecessary attention to himself. On the whole, you will see your children comfortably settling down and ready to start the day because you have filled them up emotionally.

3. **CLOSING OFF WITH A PERSONAL GAIN FOR THE DAY:**
   Letting children file out of the door without a closing remark is like baking bread without the yeast. Sometimes circumstances do not allow you to make a comment to each child as they leave the room to go home. Try saying something positive to your whole class. "Our study on insects today was exciting for me." "I sure enjoyed watching you learn today." "Your questions show that you love to learn about insects." "We can all look forward to more of this tomorrow."

   Never allow any child to go home with an unresolved conflict he encountered with you. Work it through, and again, end his day with a personal gain.

4. **INTEREST FILE:**
   Keep a "personal interest" card on each of your children. Make an effort to find out what the child does outside of school. Look through this file occasionally noting hobbies and other interests

such as sports, dance, music, videos, etc. Doing this will give you a personal connection with each child—something you can talk about together.

5. SUPPORTING INTEREST AND TALENT FILE:
When you learn of a child's interest be on the lookout for pictures, books or any learning item that relates to the specific interest or talent. For example, if you learn that Joey loves to fish, bring in a variety of fishing poles and have him add to his spelling list words that identify the fishing pole. (i.e. reel, line, drag, eyes, weight, leader.) It would be neat to present Joey with a fishing magazine or picture he could have.

6. PERSONAL CEREMONIES:
When a child in your class achieves success in any way, stop and take a few seconds to recognize this with the whole class. Use a desk, school bell or a party horn to signal to the class that someone is about to have a celebration. Show the child and his work off. Communicate your pride and respect for him.

7. NURTURING TOUCH:
Children need nurturing touch. Most children welcome it. The safest place for a child to be touched is on the upper arm. The child who finds it uncomfortable to be touched must be respected. This does not, however, mean to never touch the child again. When a child withdraws his arm or shoulder from you, do not quickly remove your hand or body from them. Keep the hand still and slowly move it away from the child. A quick, body movement away from the child communicates fear, rejection, and discomfort. Nurturing touch is not easy to give to some children. Physical closeness, without touch, may be all some children are able to handle.

8. LUNCH OR SNACK TIME WITH CHILD:
Children love to eat with their teachers. Eating with adults is a relaxing time for most children. It is a time associated with pleasure and support. If the teacher can do this with each child at least once during the school year it adds tremendously to supportive experiences at school.

All the previous suggestions are adaptable to the home environment. I will never forget a story an eighty-year old retired Army engineer told me after asking him this question: "What main event encouraged you the most to become a mechanical engineer?" This delightful man recalled a day when he brought his first, mechanical drafting layout home to share with his father. He was about ten years old at that time and had been spending time with a local drafting firm. The owner of the drafting firm sensed the boy's strong interest in mechanical drafting and let him use his tools. My friend further explained that after he showed his father the drawing his dad tacked the drawing up above the main door in the home. Whenever any visitors would come to the home his father would proudly show them his son's first mechanical drawing.

Supporting youngsters has lifelong affects. The memories of the way one is supported can be used to recover from hard times in the child's future life. A child's development is greatly influenced by the balance of support and control in his life. Control alone, without support, results in fear, resentment and often abuse. Support alone, without control instills an unrealistic picture of life for the child. On the other hand, when children experience a balance of support and control they develop high self-esteem, engage is healthy risk and are less confused about life.

CHAPTER THREE

Physical Guided Action:
Preventive Steps With The Child

When the child receives images of true character strength, he then perceives himself as capable and self-controlling.

I n most systems where people interact with one another vast amounts of resources are used for intervening after misdeeds, disputes or crimes have taken place. We witness this in our communities where large amounts of money and time are used to control undesirable behavior. Resources used for intervention, do not create long term solutions in the same way that preventive measures do. Likewise, in raising children, taking preventive steps as a method of discipline will reduce the amount of time children choose to misbehave. Preventive efforts require creativity and time on the part of the adult. In this chapter we will learn of tested, preventive measures that build self-esteem while lowering the incidence of misbehavior.

REFLECTING POSITIVE IMAGES (RPI)

RPI is a process of dissolving negative images the child has fixed within his or her mind and replacing those images with actual characteristics of inner strength. Inadequate personal experiences often negate children's real inner strengths. Children are in an ongoing process of developing their characters and personalities. When a child acts negatively towards his peers or siblings he portrays an image of himself, whether that image is true or false, to which the intervening adult responds in a negative way. The adult's response, in most situations, can act as a stimulus to anchor what the child will perceive of himself. If the adult reflects to the child that he is always the one causing trouble, he will most likely fulfill that image by being a troublemaker. On the other hand, when the child receives images of true character strength, he then perceives himself as capable and self-controlling.

When using RPI, the adult focuses on the positive character traits of the child. Stressing positive traits has positive long term effects on the child's character growth. Negative remarks have an equally devastating impact on the child as he moves into adulthood.

A positive self-image is imprinted in a child's mind by "anchoring." "Anchoring" is a method which combines physical and verbal elements to help a child commit to memory a positive or strong character trait.

Let's look at an example of a teacher using RPI in the classroom. Billy, a first-grader has an accident while playing on the bars. For safety precautions Billy is picked up by his mother and taken to the doctor. Damien, a classmate, who often has a hard time getting along with others, remarks to his teacher that he hopes Billy will be alright. Instead of the usual response of reassuring Damien that Billy will be okay his teacher chooses to reflect Damien's character as a caring and sensitive person. This might be her response:

"Damien, you have a very special gift." Damien replies by asking if the teacher has a gift for him. "No, you came to this world with this gift Damien," the teacher responds. "You are a sensitive and caring person. You care about Billy and that will mean a lot to him." As the teacher says the words "sensitive" and "caring" she gently reaches with her hand and gives Damien a squeeze on his upper arm (anchoring). Damien stops his questioning and thinks about what he has heard. More vital to Damien is the change in his self-perception from a "hard-to-get-along-with kid" to a sensitive and caring person.

RPI is also helpful when working with a child who loses control. The youngster who hits first and asks questions later needs a great deal of adult time to retrain his behavior. When working with a child like this we want to watch for and positively reflect to the slightest signs of change in the child's behavior. The changes start to come only after you, the adult, have spent time with the child trying to understand what happens to him when he gets angry. Communicate to the child what you understand about his anger and that you will not allow him to use hurtful behavior. "I value you very much as my student/child and I can't allow you to hurt yourself or others."

We may observe a child with explosive behavior raise his fist to hit a child who accidentally bumped into him. The fist, however, does not make contact with the other child. The adult using RPI responds by saying, 'I can see you were very angry John, but you really controlled yourself. You stopped and thought about it." Again the teacher anchors the image "control" with a gentle squeeze on the child's upper arm.

RPI should be an ongoing process with all children. Every child has a "caring" part of his personality. We must encourage that trait by reinforcing the behavior as we observe it.

CENTERING ON THE CHILD
It is important to distinguish between indulging the child

with too much attention and centering on the child's most important needs.

Indulging the child with too much attention is similar to inappropriate love. We think that if we offer a continuous stream of compliments that we will keep the child happy. But this type of over attention is just a means to avoid conflict. Indulgence is often a tactic used with very willful and hard to get along with children. They are happiest, we conclude, when they are made to feel superior, and self-gratified. Teachers have a tendency to call on these children frequently when they raise their hands or blurt out answers. At home, parents find themselves giving in to these children by "tip-toeing" around them and feeling frustrated and helpless.

Centering on a child's most important needs does not mean to over-indulge them with attention and undue compliments. Rather, it is a way of knowing and fulfilling the child's most specific needs by giving him our focused attention. Many times children approach us with many concerns only to be cut off by the adult who is preoccupied with a busy schedule. Too frequently we have cut the child off because we have not heard the urgency in the child's verbal message to us. A most common error is to follow the youngster's message with a message of our own. Let's look at this closer as we follow the dialogue between a child and his parent.

Child: "Mom, I don't understand why people want to rob other people."

Parent: "Billy, they're just bad people. By the way I noticed you haven't cleaned up your room yet, and your grandparents will be here in one hour."

Billy leaves his mother with a feeling that the cleanliness of his room is more important than the fear of being harmed.

With the centering process we should not let anything interfere with vital time with the child. People are often searching for assistance or reassurance throughout their lives. In the above example the child's message to his parent was never truly validated and was followed quickly by his parent's message.

DIAGRAM #1

Child	Parent
message of fear →	← **message to clean room**

Neither the child nor the parent received an acknowledgement response. The end result of this type of communication could be the child feeling overwhelmed by the fear of being harmed by others; and/or that there must be something wrong with him for feeling this way. Let's repeat this same situation with the parent centering with the child.

Child: "Mom I can't understand why people want to rob other people."

Parent: "It sounds like you've been thinking about people who hurt others."

Child: "Yes, Jimmy at school said his house was robbed over the weekend."

Parent: "Did this make you worry about our house being robbed?"

Child: "Well a little, but I know daddy can take care of us."

Parent: "You feel safe with your daddy?"

In centering, the adult truly focuses on the needs of the child by responding to the child's message of fear with understanding and compassion.

DIAGRAM #2

Child	message of fear	Parent
	message of fear →	
	response of understanding and compassion ←	
	appeal to child's need for Dad's safety-protection	

When we do not center on the child's needs we may cause him to behave inappropriately to fulfill these needs. In essense, we are teaching him to misbehave before he can truly get our full attention.

When adults cannot possibly center on the child because of a demanding schedule or situation, it is important to recognize the child's need for attention and then arrange a time when you can meet with him. Consider this situation for a teacher: You are just about ready to instruct your class and little Ray comes up and says he is worried about his home because of the heavy rains outside. Your response to little Ray might go like this:

"Ray, I can see you have something very important on your mind. I want to listen to your concerns right after I complete the instructions on our math assignment. Please be seated and I'll come to your desk soon."

Recognizing that the child has something important to tell you, and reassuring him that you will give him time allows the adult an acceptable delay. It is not harmful to temporarily delay centering on the child. Of course, going to see the child when you told him you would is extremely crucial to his wellbeing and your trusting relationship with the child.

Physical Guided Action:
The Process Used
To Treat the Misbehavior

*A true measurement of growth is evident when
the child is away from the adult's influence
and still demonstrates caring behavior.*

Physical *guided action (PGA)* is a process to assist children through misbehavior, new experiences and fears. The goals of PGA are to develop caring behavior and inner strength. The focus of the PGA process is training the child to do something better than he had done it before. There are seven steps to the PGA process. Each of them is significant toward positive character development. The steps are titled:

1. Overt ventilation (defusing emotions)
2. Action awareness (behavior used)
3. Action results (emotional affects)
4. Reconstruction (what went wrong—what can we do better)
5. Playback with new skills (redoing conflict)
6. Evaluation (how does the new skill compare with conflict behavior)
7. Consequences (natural-reasonable losses)

We will examine each of these steps thoroughly and then apply them to common intolerable behaviors as well as common fears and new experiences.

STEP ONE — OVERT VENTILATION
(defusing emotions)

Did you ever ask a child to say "sorry" to someone only to hear a half-hearted "sorreee." Elkind in his book *"The Hurried Child* refers to this as "intellectual unconscience", meaning that the child is expressing a word without any real thought to why he is saying this word. Before children can sincerely feel sorry for their actions or forgive others who have hurt them, they must first work through the feelings they have acquired from the conflict. One of the most common mistakes we have made in correcting children is to bypass unconsciously the child's need to ventilate his feelings. Overt ventilating is the first step toward assisting the child to understand his emotions, as well as the emotions of other people involved. In this step we may have to assist in helping the child find the words that describe best how he feels. Children under the age of five often do not know how to describe sadness or anger.

In a sense we are allowing the child to cleanse or "empty the barrel" with some guidance. The adult, in this crucial step, guides the child by allowing an outlet for his emotions while not permitting the emotion to determine his behavior. It is not advisable to teach children to act only upon how they feel, rather, teach them how their actions can result in something good for everyone involved.

Quite often, during this step of overt ventilation, defense mechanisms surface for the child or children involved. Defense mechanisms often divert or close off the communication process between children. For this reason, the adult secures harmony between the children by instructing that the child talking must not be interrupted.

A clear statement that will start the overt ventilation is: "Ray, I want you to describe exactly what happened to you and how you feel about what happened." The child will often describe first what the other person did to them. This should be allowed, but then followed with a request for the child to also describe what they did. If they "skirt around" their feelings by making statements like "I wish I was never Mary's friend," we can help by filling in the child's feeling for them. Adult response might go like this: "Ray are you telling us that you feel angry at Mary?" or "Could it be that you are still very angry with Mary?" If you are assisting several children, it is best to allow all of them to ventilate before progressing to the next step, action awareness.

STEP TWO — ACTION AWARENESS
(behavior used in conflict)

Following overt ventilation the adult should have a clear picture of what has happened to the child. You are now ready to give that same picture back to the child. Remember that the problem belongs to the child and not the adult. You are not going to fall into the trap of being judge or jury during this step. You want mainly to allow the child to see the overall picture of what happened. Children have a tendency to focus on self-preservation. The action awareness step provides the child with a larger scope of the conflict. This is an extremely important step in the PGA process for you are now building sensitivity and empathy for others within the child. Action awareness recalls the behavior that the child or children described to the adult. For example: "What you are describing to me is that Mary kicked you in the shins and you pushed her down. The kicking and pushing was done after Mary kicked the ball." "Is this correct?" What affect that behavior had on the child and others is our next step in the PGA process.

STEP THREE — ACTION RESULTS
(emotional affects)

Now the child is ready to see how his actions affected everyone involved in the dispute. This step continues to help instill sensitivity toward himself and others. Again we want to stay away from judging actions and simply describe what happened emotionally to each child. For example:

"Ray, when Mary kicked your ball down the court you became angry and pushed her down. When she got hurt she kicked you in the shins. This made you cry and fall down on the ground. It sounds like you both got hurt because of pushing and kicking. Is that right?" With action results the child or children are now able to step out and away from the earlier emotions and view the conflict with an objective eye. Children will accept what they have done to others when you include what has emotionally happened to them.

STEP FOUR — RECONSTRUCTION
(what went wrong—what can we do better)

When the child or children are taken through the reconstruction step they are learning new skills to handle their problem. The preceding steps have or should have established a sense of trust with the adult. The child senses fairness and a sincere desire on the part of the adult to help him. For the adults, the key skill needed here is the ability to ask questions that challenge the child to think. Most children will produce the right verbal responses about what is right and what is wrong. Most children listen to messages by adults which depict what is right and wrong and as long as the adult is present will exercise the appropriate behavior. Yet a true measurement of growth is when the child is away from the adult's influence and still demonstrates caring behavior. Our job in this phase of the PGA process is to take the child beyond the knowledge level in correcting behavior and into the action phase that reinforces that knowledge. What happens so often in the discipline process is we demand only that children tell us what is right or wrong about their behavior.

There are two new processes which will take place in a child's mind when we ask him questions which challenge him to think. First, the question should challenge the child to think of the problem as one that affected more than just himself, and second, the child should consider alternative ways to solve or cope with the problem.

You will be amazed how skillful the child can be during this step of reconstruction. The way we ask the questions should reflect a confidence in his ability to think and correct mistakes in his behavior. For example let's examine this step with the following problem:

A three-year old sister is bothering her brother when he is studying.

Mom: Billy, you told me that when you pinched your sister on her leg you were angry at her and were trying to get her to stay out of your room. Is that right?

Billy: "Yes, she wouldn't let me study for my spelling test."

Mom: "Why do you think your sister came into your room?" (getting Billy to focus on sister's needs)

Billy: "She's just a pest, she always wants to bother me."

Mom: "When your sister wants your attention she sometimes doesn't think about what you need to do. You needed peace and quiet and you were trying to tell your sister that, but she didn't do what you wanted her to." (identifying Billy's needs) "When you pinched your sister what happened to her?" (getting (Billy to think beyond his needs)

Billy: "She cried and went running to you."

Mom: "Your sister was hurt. Did the pinching help you to study better?"

Billy: "No, in fact I was worried that I was in real big trouble. Am I, Mom?" (Mom does not respond to "am I, Mom?")

Mom: "What could you do differently to get your sister to understand your need to be left alone?"

Billy: "I could tell you and maybe you could keep her company until I finish my studying."

Mom: "Okay. It sounds like you need some help with your sister. What could you do to help your sister understand that you can't play with her at that moment?"

Billy: "I can tell her that I'm studying my spelling

words and will play with her just as soon as I finish.'

What Mom could do next is to role play with Billy so that he could practice the appropriate words, and how to say those words to his sister.

During the reconstructive step children sometimes say that they do not know what to do differently. Their statement may be quite true, for many children have not learned or seen any other way to behave. Children who see adults handle problems with physical aggression often do likewise. With the statement ''I do not know'' by the child, the adult should follow with alternatives that can be used. The child is then asked to choose the alternative that he can best do. Again, we do not take over the problem.

Sometimes children say that what they did was the only thing to do, and they would do it exactly the same way next time. These children have not completed the ventilation step and are still angry or hurt. It is useless to proceed with the reconstructive step until the ventilation is completed.

STEP FIVE — PLAYBACK WITH NEW SKILLS
(redoing conflict)

''Never let the sun go down without first working out your anger'' are probably the best words to describe the playback step. The big question is how does a child go about working out his anger or conflict?

In the playback step we simply ask the child to do whatever happened before, but this time use the child's reconstructed plan. This step is not viewed upon as role playing. We take the child back to the very same location with the same people and have the child start all over again.

In the case of Billy and his three-year old sister, Mom gives him a chance to exercise his new skill. She seeks the cooperation of the younger sibling, and in essence ''turns the clock back'' so that Billy can experience a new end to the conflict. With a younger sibling we should include them in the process *after* the older sibling has acquired some skill and confidence. (Younger sibling, three years and younger often do not have the attention span to go through the PGA process, and need to be brought into the process at the playback stage.) Now Billy can use the new words and actions he has previously worked out with his mother.

There is a reassuring sense of confidence experienced by the child when going through the playback step. They now replace feelings of frustration and helplessness with a sense of self-control. The new skills, when exercised by the child, play an integral part in building the child's self-esteem. One can expect more positive behavior in the future when a child uses these skills rather than being punished and instructed never to repeat the misbehavior again.

You will probably notice a sigh of relief from the child after completing this step of the PGA process! The playback step allows for the child to feel a reduction in stress built up from the past conflict. Children who exercise these newly acquired skills receive an emotional reward, that is, the feeling of hope because they are able to work-out their problems constructively. Most children, when they describe their feeling during the heat of aggression, state that they feel and see red, feel out of control with numbness to their bodies and tremble deep inside afterwards. The playback step helps them regain control and a feeling of decency. In a sense, playback behavior is the behavior a child really wishes he could have experienced in the first place.

When children play with others who have gone through the PGA process it is noted that the child with the PGA experience was more skilled in working through a conflict. It is in the playback step when the adult should anchor the new behavior for the child with a gentle touch on the arm accompanied by words that describe strength or growth in character. The affects of the playback process are long term since they have given the child tools which are both necessary and useful for the future. The child learns by redoing something he previously learned incorrectly. The playback step also helps to reduce stress built up from the conflict.

Some children have learned to rely on severe spankings to cleanse them of feelings of guilt. There have been instances when the value of the PGA process was overshadowed by the need of troubled youth to be physically punished. This can be a dangerous emotional cycle for any child to depend upon. They may look for this same treatment from others or become self-destructive in their future relationships. The playback step focuses on what the child can do right and not on how bad the child is. In essence, we can build self-esteem in children even when they misbehave.

STEP SIX — EVALUATION
(comparing the new with the old behavior)

Once the playback step is completed we want the child to see the value of his new action and skills. We ask him to evaluate specific areas related to the conflict.

The first area the child evaluates is the *emotional affects* his new behavior had on the other person as well as himself. In Billy's case, he might realize that he did not become so angry at his sister and his sister did not get hurt. He might even conclude that he couldn't keep his sister from feeling disappointed because he couldn't play with her, but he could save her from the pain his pinching caused. The playback should give the child a measure of emotional well being, not pain.

In the second area, the child is evaluating how he met his needs. Billy had a need for being alone so that he could concentrate on his studies. The child senses that his needs are still important and can be met in a more productive manner. The needs of the child as well as the adult are important to recognize in this step. The parent can express to the child how his new behavior has a positive affect on the home situation. For example, Billy's mother might say how Billy's actions can help the family have peace and quiet after a long and tiresome work day. The evaluation step should always include anchoring (touch and words describing child's strength) the positive actions made by the child. The adult also expresses an appreciation for the child's new plan of action and the success of that plan.

The third point in evaluation is the child's comparison of the old and new behavior. The child is encouraged to describe the difference he sees in the results of both behaviors. "When you pinched your sister, what happened?" "When you talked to your sister and explained that you needed time to finish your work and would play with her later, what were the results?" These might be appropriate questions for Billy's mother to ask to help him measure the results of his new behavior.

A word of caution: After completing this step, the child might regress to statements like, "This only worked because you were here Mom, but I know sister will not mind me when you're gone." The most effective response to negative remarks is to refer the child back to what he did right. Let him know that he now has a new skill which he did not have before. You expect the child to use his new skill and will not allow him to resort back to his old, inappropriate behavior. It is best to be assertive about what you expect from the child. The child is capable of using his new skills, but often needs encouragement in assertive and reassuring ways by the adults.

The evaluation step includes feedback to the child on how he is doing with his new plan. This feedback can be as soon as fifteen minutes after going through the PGA process. Most feedback will occur at the end of the day either when the child goes to bed or leaves school for home. If a similar conflict should occur for the child and he uses even a small part of his new plan, let him know what he accomplished! It is not easy for many children to change their behavior. Children achieve positive growth in varied degrees of time. It is unrealistic to expect instant change for most children. Patience and persistence are two, important ingredients in seeing children through this process. A little prayer here and there helps too!

STEP SEVEN — CONSEQUENCES
(natural-reasonable losses)

Research indicates that the type of consequence given to a child who misbehaves is not the variable that corrects and changes his behavior. Rather, it is the consistent use of a consequence which brings about the desired change. Repeated consequences do motivate most of us to make changes in our behavior. The young child learns from approval and disapproval. The school aged child sees approval and disapproval in terms of what he can gain or lose by behaving in a certain way. For example, a youngster between the ages of five and twelve is capable of learning that appropriate behavior results in friendships, privileges and a sense of belonging. Certain behavior, the child learns, can be used to avoid pain. If you asked a nine-year old child why they should not steal, their most common response would be ''I don't want to go to jail or get a spanking.'' Even with this knowledge, children still break the rules and engage in intolerable behavior like stealing, vandalism, destroying property and physically hurting others. As adults, we want to take the child beyond the idea that appropriate behavior is used just to avoid pain.

The consequence used must fit the misbehavior. It is sad to listen to children tell me they have been removed from the baseball team because they came home late one evening. Overdoing the consequence is counterproductive to promoting positive growth in the child. When deciding on a consequence, consider the following guidelines:

1. The consequence for misbehavior should *relate to the misbehavior itself.* If the child comes home late from his friend's house, then he loses the privilege of going to anyone's house for a short period of time. If the child disturbs the peace of others at the dinner table by picking on his sibling, then he loses the privilege of eating with the family for that meal. If the child leaves his bike outside in the rain, he cannot ride the bike for a short period of time. If the child physically hurts others at school, he loses the privilege of being at school, etc. Remember: relate the consequence to the misbehavior.

2. Make consequences *short term.* It is unwise to punish children beyond a day. Long consequences teach the child ways to "break" the adult "down" and to learn new misbehavior. The extended consequence acts as a catalyst to more misbehavior. The adult then either changes her mind or over punishes the child.

3. *Consequences should be repeated.* Children often repeat misbehavior even after the PGA process. We must be careful not to give up on the consequence simply because it does not at first change the misbehavior. Children often use manuipulative statements such as "I don't care what you do" or "What good does grounding do?" etc. It is best not to allow these statements to diminish your authority over the situation. Emotionally, it is damaging for both the child and adult when the child is able to manipulate with guilt-producing statements. Stick with what you know is right for the child, and use good, common sense while managing his behavior.

4. *Put closure to consequence.* A natural adult tendency is to remind children of what happened to them the last time they engaged in a specific activity. It is common to hear parents and teachers remind their children to behave, when they are about to do something in which they previously misbehaved. These adult statements may be viewed by the child as reminders of mistrust, even after the child has gone

through the consequence with a positive attitude. The adult reminders tell the child, "I still expect you to misbehave, so I must remind you not to repeat your misbehavior before you even do it!"

It is wise to allow children the opportunity to do activities and events again even if they have previously misbehaved. The main job (and a very hard one!) is to forgive and forget. Forget to the degree that you do not badger the child for being imperfect. This effort to forgive on the adult's part facilitates positive growth in unconditional love and acceptance.

5. Consequences should allow for feedback from the child. Feedback from the child should be requested by the adult. The child is simply asked to repeat why the consequence is happening to the child. "Billy, I want you to tell me why you are losing the privilege of going on the field trip." "It's because I didn't do the preparation assignments for the field trip." "That's correct, Billy. You will be assigned to Mr. Jones class until we return." The feedback serves to reinforce the correct reasons for the consequence and to have the child hear his own words taking responsibility for his misbehavior.

In summary, applying consequences for misbehavior in children can be compared to the way shepherds, in Biblical time, tended their sheep. Whenever a sheep strayed from the flock, the shepherd used a sling and rock to get the stray sheep back to safe location in the flock. The shepherd, however, never hit the sheep with the rock. He cleverly slung the rock so that it would fall in front of the sheep's nose and direct it back to the flock. The sheep also knew the shepherd's voice; a voice which reflected care and recognition of each one individually. Sheep will never answer to the voice of a stranger. The shepherd calls sharply from time to time to remind them of his presence. The sheep know the shepherds voice, and follow it; but if a stranger calls, the sheep stop short, lift up their heads in alarm, and if it is repeated, they turn and flee. The shepherd called each sheep by name and would examine them carefully at night as they went through the gate for the night's shelter. If a sheep was injured, the shepherd would care for it immediately and never let any additional harm come to it. The shepherd also carried a short, wooden club to protect his sheep from beasts and robbers.

Although children can never be compared with sheep, it is the shepherd's manner of treatment over his sheep that is important to us. Consequences for misbehavior are not meant to physically or emotionally injure children. Rather, consequences should help teach the child a better, or more appropriate way of doing things. It is growth, and not perfection, that we should strive for in disciplining our children.

Physical Guided Action:
Its Use To Assist Children Through Fears

When children experience strength and control over what they fear they are then able to take risks safely within their environment.

F ear is experienced by all children as they become more aware of the pains and hardships of life. Fear is simply defined as a drive to terminate an unpleasant, emotional or physical state. The child, when frightened by something in his environment, tries to escape as though he were trying to escape pain. The child's lack of knowledge of how to reduce fear is complicated by his feelings of helplessness. Once children begin to fear something in their environment they will often learn to avoid all objects related to the one they fear. This avoidance can lead to insecurity and incomplete emotional growth for the child. On the other hand, when children experience strength and control over what they fear they are then able to take risks safely within their environment. The PGA process is one way through which children can learn to conquer many fears. Before we learn how to reduce fear using the PGA process, let us look at the symptoms of fear shown by children.

1. *Hyperalert* - The child suddenly moves more quickly or talks rapidly about an object or item in his immediate environment. For example, you might be walking through a neighborhood where a dog suddenly appears and your child may quickly grab your hand, walk quicker, or want to be held. The child may begin talking too much and have difficulty listening to what you are saying. This is why our voices of reassurance are not always productive in settling the child down.

2. *Overdependency* - This symptom of fear is characterized by the child's clinging to the adult. At school, this behavior might be shown by the child's constant desire to be close to the teacher, holding his or her hand or constantly wanting the teacher's full attention. At home the child may be frightened to go to sleep each night, and only want to be where his parents are. Overdependent children avoid areas in their lives which they are truly ready to handle because fear overtakes their sense of confidence. Overdependency on the adult is often a learned behavior by the child. Too much adult protection during the early stages of a child's development can delay the development of inner strength. As children become more knowledgeable about the painful or harmful aspects of life (death of parents, kidnapping, etc.) they, hopefully, have had some experiences behind them which have fostered some

independence. When we deny the child the experience of sleeping by themselves, for example, and quickly comfort them every time they cry before they fall asleep, we make them too dependent on external comforts. As children develop they must be allowed to experience difficult times to help prepare them for later years. The child cannot sleep with his parents when he is ten years old, so he should not be sleeping with them when he is two. Overprotective anticipation by the parent of the child's needs may cause distress, anger, confusion and rage to surface later on. These emotions are real in everyone's life; we must learn how to handle them and not allow them to manifest into fear.

POOR CONCENTRATION AND MEMORY

Concentration can be affected by a child's preoccupation with fear. If a child feels inadequate in terms of his performance in school, he has little or no energy to concentrate on assignments. Communication between child and teacher is hindered when a child feels anxious or fearful regarding failure. You, as teacher, may be assisting a child with a math skill and witness that he did not understand a thing you have said. Fear can program the child's mind to fail before he even starts an assignment. Other symptoms connected with poor memory and concentration are overt physical behaviors such as a quavering voice, headaches, episodes of hyperventilation, abdominal pain, muscle tension, frequent urination, and nausea.

THE PGA PROCESS AND FEAR

It is rewarding to observe a child escape from the capsule of fear. The child's relief allows him to enjoy life more freely. On the following pages I will work through with you the most common fears experienced by children. The PGA steps are very much the same as described in the previous chapter. Describing the PGA process in the treatment of fears will be done in case form giving the reader a model for what words and attitudes can be used.

Nightmares

Three year-old Billy screams out, waking up his mother and the rest of the family. When mother walks into Billy's room she turns on the light and sees Billy sitting up wide-eyed and crying. Billy explains that there is a monster in his room with large eyes and teeth trying to catch him. Mom encourages Billy to describe what he was doing in the dream. Billy explains that every time he used a stick to scare the monster away the monster would eat the stick up. Mom responds by saying, "The monster really frightened you because you thought he was going to eat you too." "Yes, mommy, I couldn't run away either." "Is the monster still in this room, Billy?" mother asked with sincerity. Billy hesitantly says, "I'm not sure, but I don't want him to come back." "Well, Billy, we can either make friends with this monster or chase him out of your room forever." "Lets make friends with the monster," Billy urges. "Okay, let's look around and find out where the monster could be." "Oh mommy, look, there he is underneath my bed," Billy says as he grabs mom's hand tightly. "By golly, he sure is Billy, and you were right. He has big eyes. Let's let him know we won't hurt him." Billy tells the monster, "We won't hurt you. What's your name? He doesn't have a name, mom." "What should we name him, Billy? I know, he looks like Elmer Fudd! So let's name him Elmer. Hi, Elmer!" mother initiates, with Billy repeating the same greeting. Mom reaches to the monster and pets him on the head and describes how soft his fur feels. She invites Billy to do the same and he carefully reaches to the supposed monster. "Look how he blinks his eyes. I think he likes us. Oh golly, it looks like Elmer has to go home. He could only visit for a little while. Good-bye, Elmer," Mom says and again Billy repeats mom's words with, "Good-bye, Elmer."

Mom tucks Billy back in bed, gives him a big kiss and tells him how happy she is that Billy is her boy. With nightmares we should physically take the child through an experience that leaves them feeling inner strength.

As early as one or two years old, children begin dreaming. At this age children do not have a vocabulary to describe the details of their dreams, so they cry out in fear. As children enter their school age years they are well-equipped to verbalize their dreams and pick out details that frighten them. By following the child's verbalization of the nightmare with physical action you are reassuring the child he is stronger than the dream portrayed him to be.

If your child experiences many nightmares it is best to take preventive steps to lessen the nightmares. Sometimes a fear producing source are the posters hung in your child's room. Posters of fierce looking animals can trigger the nightmare. Also, check to see if your child is filling up his day with too many activities (even happy ones.) Are there too many expectations placed on your child's performance at school or at home? Your child should definitely be guarded from gory details of the tragedies in life. Believe it or not, the local TV news is full of frightening scenes for our children. Movies that include violence and human torture should be entirely avoided by everyone. Most children do not realize that they dream at all because they never remember their dreams unless they wake up. In essence, waking up after a bad dream is purposeful. It is a time when the child can recall much detail. Verbalizing a nightmare can lead to understanding it and conquering the fears it produces. This is achieved more quickly with a supportive parent using the PGA process.

Dreams are initiated biochemically by serotonin and norepinephrine, the same brain amines that when depleted result in clinical depression. If we make fun of the child or deprive him of the full experience of working through the anguish or fear within those nightmares, we may force him into feelings of inadequacy. We know that when people hold grudges or seek extreme revenge they deplete these essential brain amines. I believe it is possible that children can also deplete these essential amines when nightmares are not handled carefully, perhaps causing them to experience mild depression.

Dreams, as well as nightmares, have a purpose in the child's development. Nightmares are part of a process where children resolve unconscious conflicts, or at least dissipate some of the emotional pain tied to events which caused conflict or confusion during the day.

FEAR OF GOING TO NEW ENVIRONMENTS
(school, homes, etc.)

Dad comes home and announces that he has been transferred to a new location in another town. Becky, his ten-year old daughter, breaks down in tears and says that she will lose all of her friends. She also says she loves her present home which has been a part of her life since she was born. Dad allows her to express her future losses without making statements like, "Oh heck, Becky, you'll make new friends," or "A house is just a house and we will find another one." All members of the family are allowed to express their feelings of loss, even Dad. There is a time of holding one another and verbal reassurance. Dad, later on, initiates a time of talking about all the unforgettable special events that took place at their present home. Becky laughs as dad recalls the day when she, at three, helped him thin the corn plants in the family garden. They walk out to the plot where Becky left only one plant in each row of corn. Dad continues talking about other special events that took place. He allows Becky to verbalize her feelings and to collect one thing from each of these special places to take with her before they leave.

Becky is now in her new home and the fear of going to her new school surfaces to a conscious level. Her voice quivers when she talks about going to the new school and many questions are asked. "I wonder if the teacher will be nice?" "Will the kids be friendly?" "Will the work be too hard for me?" etc. Dad suggests that they both walk to school and look it over. Dad purposely walks to school because that's the way Becky will have to travel. Dad and Becky stroll throughout the school grounds to find her classroom, play area, restroom and the main office. Becky wants to play on the bars for a while and dad watches. They walk back home together and share with mom what the new school is like. Dad lets Becky do all the talking, observing some optimism in her voice for the first time. Dad points out how well she found her classroom and other important areas. Becky wonders how she is going to make friends at her new school. Dad asks Becky to remember a time when she made a friend at her previous school. She describes that she just started to learn people's names. Dad encourages the use of Becky's social skills by pretending he is a student at Becky's new school. Becky practices her skills with Dad. Dad realizes that this practice reinforces the inner strength Becky needs to meet her new challenge. Becky asks, "What should I do if I get scared or feel lonely at the new school?" Dad asks her if she can think of someone who makes her feel safe when she is with that person. Becky says, "Mom and Dad." Dad firmly, but empathetically states that Mom and Dad cannot be with her at school, and asks, "Where can you keep a memory of Mom and Dad?" Becky thinks for a while and says, "In my heart." Dad tells Becky that if she should feel scared or lonely on her first day at school she only needs to touch her heart and remember that Mom and Dad are always there.

When adults make changes in their children's environment it is important to assist them in adapting to new elements such as school, neighborhood and even friends. Some children adapt easier than others, but it is unwise to assume that all children are durable and emotionally tough when facing multiple change. Many children protect their parents from their fears of change because they can sense the hardship that parents are experiencing. The best "rule of thumb" is to always assist children when making major changes in their environment.

The preceding description of a method to handle Becky's transition to a new home and school can be used in many, different situations. Going to the dentist or doctor can be handled in the same manner. Most doctors and dentists would gladly assist you in gradually building your child's inner strength before their actual visits.

FEAR OF GOING TO SCHOOL

Often, as parents and educators, we have children who have "turned school off" very early in life. The child's resistance to encouragement and support frustrates us to the point of using "hard nose" techniques to "motivate" the child to want to attend or do well in school. Our most common mistake in these situations is to focus on the symptoms or outward behavior of the child rather than on the causes for the behavior. Symptoms are coded messages of what may be repressed by the child. In a sense, the child's outward emotions give the world a glimpse of what is happening internally. With patience and careful examination of what the child is saying with resistant behavior, we can find the most desirable way to assist the child.

The average parent and teacher tries harder when the child "turns school off." In these cases, adults often see themselves in the child they are frustrated with. Instead of saying, "I must try differently," they say, "I must try harder." Unfortunately, this response to the child intensifies the fear and or anger related to school. Following are some recommended PGA steps for working with the child who is resisting school.

Step 1. The adult must first deal with their own emotions before assisting in the child.

Much frustration and energy go into the resistant child. A frightened and angry child intensifies his resistance when an adult is angry with him. When the adult is angry at the child, the child cannot freely express his feelings, and these channels for building internal strength are closed off. So, our first step is to examine and care for our own emotions and needs.

Adults' statements to gain self-control:
1. "My child is hurting inside and I hurt for him, too."
2. "I feel hurt because I care so much for my child."
3. "To my knowledge I have done the very best I can and I am going to stay with this child."
4. "This child needs me, and I am now ready to take the next step to understand what my child says he really needs."

Step 2. Determine the reason or cause behind the resistance to attend school.

a. "The child that *won't* and says he really *can't*." Your child, in this case, is saying indirectly "I am scared to expose myself." It is frightening for him to truly say I feel inadequate in the learning environment at school. The child may be using passive resistance to protect his faltering self-image. He is often capable of succeeding in school but sabotages any movement forward. An outward clue is that the child may take on a helpless or assumed helpless attitude toward school. The adult often feels sorry for the child and wants to rescue him.

b. The child that won't and says he really *"won't."* This child may be suffering from problems outside of school, such as divorce, abandonment, death and other changes that have suddenly broken his sense of security. In these cases, the child often uses resistant behavior to get back at adults. An outward clue may be obnoxious behavior causing the adult to feel angry at the child.

In both *a.* and *b.* the children are most likely capable of achieving in school, but need help with emotional issues in their lives. The best direction is to find out what those issues are.

c. "The child that *can't* and says he *won't*." This child is most likely "saving face." He first appears to be a child who is being belligerent and uncooperative, The underlying truth is that the child is having a hard time saying he needs help. He feels he is letting you down and is scared he may be mentally inferior. The outward clue is similar to the child who "won't and says he won't." The way we distinguish between these two children is to present the child with something we know he can do. The child who "won't and says he won't" will refuse to perform. The child who "can't and says he won't" usually will perform the task because he wants you to perceive him as being capable. When a child refuses by "saving face" he is protecting an inner desire to be accepted by the adult.

d. The child that *"can't* and says he *can't."* This child is usually being honest with the adult. He often has a poor self-image and exercises negative self-thought. The outward clue is usually confusion about school work and verbal direction. The adult feels worried and responds by maintaining a genuine interest in assisting the child.

Step 3. Take the child through the PGA process.

A *gradual* approach to reduce resistance toward school is recommended. Once we have determined the cause(s) for the child's resistance, we can then assist him to build inner strength, and achieve success over the problem. Let us first approach this process by examining a case where the child is quite capable of achieving in school but suddenly refuses to go to school.

I would like to introduce you to Jenny, a sixth grader, who is attending a school where she has been a student since kindergarten. It is two weeks into the new school year and Jenny has refused to go to school. Her parents describe her behavior as sad and complaining. It all started with complaining that her stomach hurts. The parents chose to keep her home for two days after her first complaints of ill health. After seven days of absence from school Jenny continued to complain about not feeling well. The parents suggested that something more than physical illness was involved. At that point they insisted that she go to school When she was being driven to school she became "so sick." When she began to complain that she was going to vomit, mom turned around and took Jenny back home. As soon as the car went in the opposite direction of school the violent symptoms subsided. Jenny was quiet.

Mom's next step, in this case, should be to deal with her own emotions, for she has become impatient and angry at herself for letting her daughter talk her out of going to school. Mom now has Jenny sit with her to talk about what is making her too scared to go to school. (overt ventilation). Mom's patient and compassionate manner allows Jenny the freedom to express that she is scared to leave her parents, even to go to school. Further explanation reveals that since her grandmother died she has been afraid her parents might die, too. Jenny felt this way because both parents had been preoccupied in caring for the dying grandparent.

With this new information, mother was able to explain to her daughter that her refusal to go to school was a direct result of her grandmother's death, and the lack of time spent with mom and dad during her grandmother's illness. (Action awareness).

Mother asked Jenny to tell her what the desire to be absent from school meant to her. Jenny stated that she was afraid to leave her mother because she was scared she would die. The next, and important message that came from Jenny was that she wanted to regain closeness to her parents that she did not feel during her grandmother's illness. (Action results).

Mother then knew that the cause of Jenny's resistance to school was directly related to a long break in the nurturing Jenny normally received from her family. Mother wisely hugged Jenny and planned a time, after school, where they could go for a walk together. Jenny still responded with some resistance to go to school, but it was more in a question, "Do I really have to go to school, mom?" rather than the direct refusal she expressed earlier. Mother, with Jenny, decided how much time Jenny could handle tomorrow at school. Jenny stated two hours and mom countered with one hour. Mother's reduction of time was to insure total success at school and with the separation from home. (Reconstruction).

Mother and Jenny then took a drive to school to gradually build her strength back into her school environment. When they came home they talked about how the drive felt. Jenny was elated about her success at getting that close to school and not panicking. The next day Jenny went to school for one hour and mom picked her up. Jenny again described her success at being at school. (Evaluation of new plan). On the second day Jenny increased her stay at school by fifteen minutes. When her mother came to pick her up Jenny wanted to stay the whole day. From this point on Jenny regained her strength to detach from home and had conquered her fear successfully.

FEAR OF GOING TO BED

Not all resistance toward going to bed is related to fear. More frequently, problems in the area of bedtime are related to learned behavior. It is true that some children resist bedtime because they are afraid of imagined monsters or supposed danger coming upon them. Since I have already addressed this issue earlier in the chapter, I will now discuss negative learned behavior, resistance to bedtime and the PGA process.

How do children learn to resist going to bed? Many children at a very early age, six to eight months, learn to depend on the comforts provided by mom or dad prior to bedtime. A parent's touch and voice are comforts which are healthy for children. It is the saturation of these comforts that begin a dependency on external stimuli and resistance to self-relaxation and sleep. It is common knowledge that the more we go to the child every time she whines after placing her in bed, the more she needs attention at bedtime. We want our children to be safe and comfortable. Their cry for comfort motivates our response to care for the child. This is not an abnormal adult behavior, but we tend to overdo our job sometimes! The hardest thing for parents to do is to let their children cry themselves to sleep. When we have determined that our child's crying is merely a plea for more of our time and not a cry of pain, we can then follow the prescribed PGA plan.

Let us say that your child at eight to eleven months is constantly whining for you to return to her bedside. As you enter the room you notice your child, standing with pleading eyes and arms stretched out to you. You have two choices: One is to pick up the child and rock her back to sleep each time she cries throughout the night; or you may place the child back on the mattress, cover her, and give her a pat on the head; then when you determine that your child is perfectly fine, do not return again. The first option teaches resistance to bedtime. Returning to comfort the child when the problem is not comfort, but a demand for attention, encourages further bedtime resistance. Option one actually responds to the adult's needs. In this case it is clearly the adult who is uncomfortable. The child is perfectly fine but wants more of a good thing. The adult, on the other hand, feels more at ease when the child is quiet and resting.

Providing safe play items in the crib is a good solution for children (between eight and eleven months) who resist bedtime. With some diversion they can entertain themselves and finally go back to sleep. If they wake and cry for the adult, this crying will continue for a certain period of time. The crying time will decrease as the child learns that the adult will not take charge of the child's ability to relax and fall asleep. The purpose is to equip the child to handle periods of arousal from sleep independently rather than to rely on a parent.

If you are experiencing bedtime problems with a school-ages child, you should first examine the bedtime routine. You may want to ask yourself the following questions:
1. Do I have a regular deadline for going to bed, or does this vary from night to night?
2. Does my child put himself to sleep?
3. Do I spend some time with my child at his bedside (prior to sleep)? If so, what are we doing?
4. Do I read to my child?

The school-aged child needs a consistent bedtime routine. An important element in the routine is to end TV viewing well before the child is to go to bed. Television viewing for children can stimulate their adrenalin flow. The child's energy reserve system can be activated to the point of vigorous physical and mental activity. Children need a period of time to reduce the amount of energy caused by many of the television programs. The hour before bedtime should include quiet nurturing activities. Following is a recommended bedtime ritual that could eliminate the problems of getting children to go to bed. First, establish a time for going to bed on school nights. Let us say that this time is 8:15 p.m., sharp!

7:30   Television is turned off for the whole family. The reason for this is to establish quality in the

	parent-child time together.
7:30-7:40	Give the children a chance to talk over what they saw on television. There may be scenes that need to be talked about. Use this time to sort out TV and family values and what is, or what is not reality. Careful selection of TV viewing is a stress preventive procedure that must take place in all homes.
7:40-7:50	Each family member tells of one new thing they learned that day. This time is specifically used to give focused attention to each other and build communication skills together.
7:50-8:10	Preparation for bedtime and the next school day. A time for brushing teeth and laying out clothes, books, etc. for the next day.

Storytime. The bedtime story is so important to the child. The child's reading skills and imagination are most affected by being read to at early ages. Bedtime stories should be a part of every child's bedtime up to ten years of age. It is my belief that if parents can diligently and faithfully read to their children up to the age of ten, their children will value and continue reading into adulthood. Reading, among other things, enhances intellectual growth and enjoyment. In other words, books become more valuable and enjoyable than TV. Children will also be better readers and comprehend what they read beyond the present national norms. This is especially valuable for the child who may have a learning disability. The positive experiences with books for the learning disabled child increases their courage to pursue the small levels of academic growth they normally experience in school.

| | |
| 8:10 | The day now ends with a special message. The family members tell each other something special about one another. Prayer follows, using this special message to communicate appreciation to God. Remember to conclude all days with conflicts resolved. Never allow yourself or your child to go to sleep without |

first resolving all conflicts that might have occurred during the day.

The preceding bedtime routine can vary with each family and its needs. If you look closely at the recommended procedure it focuses on calming children down through close involvement with their family. We do know that children in the nineteen eighties are starving for quality time with adults. As you design your bedtime routine and ritual keep in mind that you are not only calming your child down, but also providing positive experiences that will last a lifetime.

FEAR OF DYING

The fear of death starts early in a child's life. Many psychologists believe the trauma of birth and the entrance into a hostile world may be the first step towards death anxiety. The first moment the child leaves the uterus he must fight to survive. The infant is totally helpless and dependent on his providers. As the child matures past infancy he will experience various degrees of separation from his mother. It is possible that these early experiences of separation develop a fear of separation which may grow into a submerged fear of death. Mothers are a vital source of security and protection for the child. Children often seek their mother's love as a protection against injury, pain and death.

The way parents treat their infant child emotionally is vitally important as it influences the child's view of death. For example, if a parent rejects the child by withholding love, the child then fears the loss of his own life. The child views this as abandonment. Much of the infant's fear of death is submerged and is not realized until the child is able to understand that a cause will produce an effect. Clearly, before the concept of death is understood by children, they must be able to consciously organize experiences and mentally arrange these experiences into explainable causes. Children witness death of pets, plants and people. Once the cause and affect concept is realized by the child, then, and only then, do they consciously fear death.

Children easily sense the difficulty parents and teachers have in discussing death. Often adults equate death with old age to ease the child's worry. The child, however, is mentally equipped to understand that people start by being young and then get old. To the child this means that mom and dad will get old, too. Thoughts about one's parents dying arouse anxiety and confusion for the child. Society, as a whole, represses the concept of death. Children find themselves fearing death, but often have no outlet to express the fear. Death anxiety in children, indeed, is influenced by cultural values and behaviors. exhibited by the child's parents and extended family. If in fact, the child is taught that death is something evil, or something we try to eradicate in our lives, we instill either intense outward fear or a subconscious unrealistic desire for immortality.

PGA PROCESS: The first step in assisting children with understanding death is to teach them that death is real and fear of its threat is completely rational. Second, we want to counter what society teaches about death. We want to teach that fear of death is a sign of maturity and strength. Our third and final step is to aid the child to overcome his present worry or anxiety and not to dwell on or cultivate it to a neurotic state. Overcoming fear seems to be best facilitated by an avenue for physical release, for example, allowing the child to care for something he values. It is important to teach a child about involvement with and service to others during life.

Let us go through the PGA process together with a loss felt by many children: the death of a grandparent. Using the following dialogue between the child and adult we will demonstrate the use of the PGA process in assisting children with death. The funeral is over and the eight-year old Johnny has gone through the harsh reality of losing a very special person in his life for the first-time. The child has withheld any questions about death knowing that the rest of his family has been grieving. We notice that Johnny's behavior has had some sudden changes. We observe these symptoms:

1. Forgets to do things for himself that he did easily and consistently before (child may still be in shock over loss. His mind may seem to be somewhere else.)
2. Shallowness of breath.
3. Child appears to be tired alot.
4. The child cannot go to sleep, fears the night time and wants to sleep with parents.
5. Loss of appetite.
6. Child makes statements like: "I have a tightness in my throat!", "My stomach hurts!", "I can't sleep!", "Who

will be my Grandpa now?''
7. The child is hostile towards friends and siblings.
8. The child blames others easily.
9. The child projects a hopeless, unhappy disposition towards life in general.
10. The child may assume mannerisms of the deceased person.
11. Regressive changes in behavior.
12. Poor bowel and bladder control.
13. Child becomes hyperactive.
14. Prolonged loss of ability to concentrate.
15. Cries easily.

We will now follow the interaction between the parent and child.

Child: ''Why did Grandpa have to die anyway?''
Adult: ''His body was so sick it was not able to give him a happy life anymore.''
Child: ''What happens to Grandpa now?''
Adult: ''Grandpa is no longer sick or in pain.''
''Grandpa believed he would be with God and wanted us not to worry about him.''
Child: ''Do all people have to die when they get old?''
Adult: ''Everyone will die someday. Grandpa died when he was eighty years old. He lived a happy life.''
Child: ''Will you die someday too, like Grandpa?''
Adult: ''Yes, I will die someday too.''
Child: ''Who will take care of me?''
Adult: ''You will most likely be able to take care of yourself. If I should die before you grow up I have arranged for Aunt Mary to take care of you.''

We should allow the child to ask all the questions he needs to. Our responses should be honest, sensitive and accepting of the child's feelings. Always answer the child's questions instead of putting them off by telling them they are too young. Try not to put up barriers that may inhibit the child's attempts to communicate. Do consider the age of the child you are assisting. From the age of ten through adolescence, children begin to realize that death is a one-way process that is inevitable. Avoid the use of euphemisms such as ''Grandpa has gone to sleep." (This may result in sleeping problems.) God is a big part of the healing connected in such a way that the child may become angry with or fearful of God. Avoid statements like: "It was God's will and He took your Grandpa away." In this ventilation skill, the adult's success in helping the child to cope with death is directly related to his own ability to cope. When you feel the child has asked all the questions about death, link the child back to his reasons for living.

Adult: "Johnny, what do you remember most about being with Grandpa?"

Child: "I remember how much fun it was to go fishing with him. He always sang a little song to encourage the fish to bite. We laughed so much together."

Adult: "Would you like to go fishing with me like you did with Grandpa?" (Linking child back to living.)

Child: "Gee, yea I would. Could we go where Grandpa always took me?"

Adult: "We sure can. That's a place that you can continue to go fishing at any time."

At this point in the PGA process you want to reflect positive images to the child. Tell him that he had the courage and maturity to talk about a very painful experience. You, too, had the strength to assist the child during a painful period. Amazing as it is, when the adult is able to courageously work with the child, he can help himself toward personal healing.

Adult: "Johnny, your questions about Grandpa's death shows that you have courage and strength." (Reach out and gently touch your child on the shoulder or arm to anchor the image of strength.)

At this stage of the PGA process we want to involve the child in some type of care over something the child values. In a sense, we are repeating the connection to living, but adding an important object to care for. You need to know the child's interests to help in deciding what should be given to the child to care for. Often, I have given children one of my stuffed teddy bears to take home and care for until they feel a reduction of fear. Following are some things a child might value that will aid the healing process:

1. Plant and care for flowers.
2. Care for stuffed animal.
3. Invite a friend to stay overnight.
4. Plant a tree in the forest.
5. Make something for someone at home or school.
6. Help to bake cookies, cake or dinner.
7. Write a letter to someone who needs encouragement.
8. Draw a picture for someone.
9. Send a tape recorded message to someone special.

Early, positive death education is essential for children. Often the education process seems to begin after the child experiences the loss of a pet or relative. Statistics show that one out of five students will experience a parent's death during his or her school years.* The PGA process may be a helpful method of assisting a child. There are many agencies such as Hospice that can support family and children. If an adult recognizes that it is too painful to assist a child with the fear of death, it is advised that they refer the child to a supportive agency.

*Death Education (Washington, D.C. Hemisphere Publishing Corp., 1978), p. 295

CONCLUSION

Fear knocked at the door
Faith answered it
Nothing was there

Raising our children will be the most profound task we will have in our lifetime. It will be our faith in God and then in ourselves that will help us to endure the times we feel the most frustration and frightened. It will not be easy but every ounce of energy devoted to helping our children learn right from wrong, will bring our world closer to the true meaning of love.

The Physical Guided Action process is one approach that I feel will give adults another tool to assist children. It is not all inclusive and it is not a cure for all misbehavior. It has been used and tested in my work with children and parents with many satisfactory results. I share it with you with the hopes that it will bring you closer to the children in your life.